Paranormal Activity

Other titles in *The Mysterious & Unknown* series:

The Mysterious  & Unknown

Paranormal Activity

by Patricia D. Netzley

ReferencePoint Press®

San Diego, CA

©2012 ReferencePoint Press, Inc.
Printed in the United States

For more information, contact:
ReferencePoint Press, Inc.
PO Box 27779
San Diego, CA 92198
www.ReferencePointPress.com

LIBRARY OF CONGRESS CATALOGING-IN-PUBLICATION DATA

Netzley, Patricia D.
  Paranormal activity / by Patricia D. Netzley.
    p. cm. — (The mysterious & unknown)
  Includes bibliographical references and index.
  ISBN-13: 978-1-60152-240-5 (hardback)
  ISBN-10: 1-60152-240-1 (hardback)
 1. Spirits—Juvenile literature. I. Title.
  BF1461.N483   2012
  133.9—dc23
                                                                2011037757

CONTENTS

FOREWORD

Since the beginning of recorded history, people have been perplexed, fascinated, and even terrified by events that defy explanation. While science has demystified many of these events, such as volcanic eruptions and lunar eclipses, some remain outside the scope of the provable. Do UFOs exist? Are people abducted by aliens? Can some people see into the future? These questions and many more continue to puzzle, intrigue, and confound despite the enormous advances of modern science and technology.

It is these questions, phenomena, and oddities that Reference-Point Press's *The Mysterious & Unknown* series is committed to exploring. Each volume examines historical and anecdotal evidence as well as the most recent theories surrounding the topic in debate. Fascinating primary source quotes from scientists, experts, and eyewitnesses as well as in-depth sidebars further inform the text. Full-color illustrations and photos add to each book's visual appeal. Finally, source notes, a bibliography, and a thorough index provide further reference and research support. Whether for research or the curious reader, *The Mysterious & Unknown* series is certain to satisfy those fascinated by the unexplained.

INTRODUCTION

Frightening Forces

While staying overnight in a motel in Albuquerque, New Mexico, in February 2001, 20-year-old Nora and her 19-year-old best friend, Brooke, were startled when the television turned on by itself. They turned it off, but it turned back on and began changing channels as its volume went up and down. Suspecting they were the victims of a prank, the girls unplugged the TV and left the room with the intention of finding another motel. But because it was late at night and they were tired, they quickly decided to give the place another try.

When they returned to the room, the TV turned back on, and they discovered that it was plugged in again. Then the lights in the room flickered on and off. Now the women became afraid, suspecting that something supernatural was going on.

They decided to read aloud from the Bible, thinking it would drive away any evil spirits. Sure enough, nothing strange happened while they were reading, and eventually they decided it was safe to go to sleep. But once the lights were out, they heard awful noises coming from the bathroom, as though a wolf were snarling, growling, and howling in there. They fled the room and slept in the car.

Another Confrontation

The next morning the girls convinced themselves to go back into the room to take a shower. "We started to think about ghost movies," Nora later explained, "and thinking, well, nothing ever happens in the day."[1] To be safe, they decided to take turns. One of them showered while the other stood near the doorway waiting to run for help at the slightest sign of trouble. Brooke went into the shower first. A few minutes later she came running out, naked and screaming, insisting she had been pummeled by a shampoo bottle that left a mark on her forehead.

Nora decided to give the shower a try, telling herself the shampoo bottle must have struck her friend by accident. But as she was shampooing her long hair, she, too, was attacked. "I felt somebody grab my hair," she reported, "twist it, and then wind it around their wrists . . . and then it yanked back and I actually had some hair ripped out. There was nothing my hair could've caught on, there were no handles and the shower nozzle wasn't in the right area."[2] She, too, ran out of the shower screaming, and the two quickly left the motel.

People who believe that the spirits of the dead can attack the living would say that Nora and Brooke were victims of an angry ghost, perhaps that of someone who had died in that motel room. In fact, Nora later told Jeff Belanger, an expert on the supernatural who interviewed her for his book *Our Haunted Lives: True Life Ghost Encounters*, that her motel experience made her a believer in ghosts. This experience was, she said, "something you just can't discount."[3]

Belanger reports that Nora's reaction is typical. "Do you trust your own senses? Most of us do," he says. "And the people [I've interviewed] do as well. Some used to say, 'I won't believe unless I see it,' and see it they did. [So] there was truth and conviction in the retelling."[4]

Belanger says that such experiences are so powerful that they create equally powerful memories. "Do you remember what you got for a present on your fifth birthday? Probably not. But do you remember your child being born? The death of a loved one? Your wedding day? These are profound events, and they've been burned into your long-term memory. The ghost encounter is no different. Whether 5 years or 50 years have gone by, the experience is still vivid."[5]

Skeptics would not call such experiences ghost encounters. Instead they would dismiss them as the result of an overactive imagination, a hallucination, or a vivid dream. These experiences usually occur late at night when those encountering the "ghost" are extremely tired. Skeptic Robert T. Carroll argues that the time of day affects the way people perceive ghostly events. In his book *The Skeptic's Dictionary for Kids*, he says:

> Why do ghosts show up only at night or in dark places? Why should ghosts care whether it is day or night? They don't have to work or go to bed early so they'll be fresh for school the next day. . . . The imagination is more likely to run wild in the dark than in the sunlight. Things always seem more mysterious at night. Many people are afraid of the dark because they can't see what's really going on around them. Fear is fuel for the imagination.[6]

Residual Hauntings

But believers point out that ghost encounters have also occurred in daylight, especially in places associated with death, such as cemeteries, battlefields, and locations where brutal murders have

Sights, sounds, and smells—echoes of past events—have been reported in cemeteries in broad daylight. This type of paranormal activity is known as a residual haunting.

Paranormal Activity

occurred. One of the most prominent examples of such a place is the Barclay Cemetery, which is all that remains of the once thriving coal-mining town of Barclay Mountain, Pennsylvania. Almost all visitors to this cemetery claim to hear the sound of pickaxes hitting rocks as they walk among the gravestones—as though the dead are still digging for coal.

Ghost hunters—people who study ghost-related phenomena—call this type of paranormal activity a residual haunting. The experience seems to involve echoes from an earlier time—sights and sounds and perhaps even smells that repeat over and over again. In many instances, the person experiencing the residual haunting was not present at the original time or event. Sometimes the sight or sound or smell that repeats is a routine event, like mining. More often, though, it represents a traumatic event.

For example, numerous residual hauntings have been reported in the Tower of London. This monument, built at the beginning of the eleventh century and expanded over time into a fortified complex, was the site of many executions and various other sordid events from history. One residual haunting tale features the ghost of the fifth wife of King Henry VIII, Catherine Howard, who was imprisoned in the Tower in 1541. She escaped her room the day before she was to be beheaded for treason and ran screaming for help, but she was quickly caught. Since then many people have apparently seen her ghost repeating this experience in the hallway where it originally took place. Ghost hunters say this is because such spots hold residual energy from the death that occurred there. As the website of Wexford Paranormal, a ghost-hunting company based in Wexford Town, Ireland, explains, "Residual hauntings are no more than an expression or manifestation of stored energy."[7]

Experts in ghost phenomena differentiate this type of experi-

ence from ones involving "living ghosts," which are described as ghosts that interact with people and the real-world environment. Called an intelligent or interactive haunting, this experience features the kind of paranormal activity that Nora and Brooke apparently came across. It involves an active rather than passive spirit—one that has the ability to change television channels and volume, for example, and mount a physical attack on a person. In other cases, living ghosts have been said to move objects around and try to communicate with people. Their presence can sometimes be felt by a temperature change in the room (usually a noticeable chill) or by the appearance of a sound or smell associated with the deceased (such as the scent of a favorite perfume).

Millions of Reports

Both residual and intelligent hauntings have been reported since ancient times in many parts of the world. Recent surveys have shown that roughly one-fifth of Americans claim to have seen or sensed the presence of a ghost. In fact, by some estimates, ghost encounters throughout history number in the millions. This, believers say, should be ample proof that ghosts are real.

Some paranormal researchers say that ghost encounters are real experiences but the ghosts that people see or hear are not necessarily spirits of the dead. Perhaps some other mysterious force is creating the paranormal activity being witnessed, a force that has yet to be discovered. As ghost hunter John Kachuba notes in his book *Ghosthunters*, often the first explanation for a phenomenon is not the correct one:

> Thousands of years ago, early man felt the earth tremble and quake, saw it split open before his very eyes, and believed those actions to be caused by

Spectral Sails

For well over 200 years, during a few nights in late fall, a ghost ship has been spotted in Canada's Northumberland Strait from the shores of the fishing village of Merigomish on one side of the strait and Prince Edward Island on the other. The three-masted schooner appears out of nowhere, moving rapidly in a northeasterly direction with its sails unfurled before seeming to run aground. Many witnesses then see the shadows of people running back and forth on the deck as the ship's sails catch fire. Some say they have seen the people jumping overboard as flames engulf the ship; others describe seeing only the flames. In either case, once the ship is fully ablaze it plunges into the sea or simply vanishes.

Hundreds of people have seen the burning ship but no one knows what causes the recurring images or what ship these images might represent. Some say the schooner is the ghost of a pirate vessel said to have sunk in the area centuries ago at around the same time of year. Others say that sightings result from a trick of the autumnal light combined with people seeing what they expect to see based on stories they have heard.

angry gods, rather than sliding tectonic plates. The Ancient Chinese saw the sun disappear from the sky during an eclipse and believed that a dragon had swallowed it. . . . It may be that the weird and sometimes frightful actions we attribute to ghosts may simply be the palpable manifestations of some scientific principles we do not yet understand.[8]

Kachuba cites a possible alternate explanation for ghosts. This theory is that ghosts "exist because we *will* them to exist. . . . It may be possible that people who have suffered the loss of someone dear to them . . . could create ghosts in their own minds that appear to them as very real beings."[9] A similar theory is that whether or not they have suffered a loss, some people have psychic powers that enable their subconscious minds to create paranormal activity.

According to recent surveys, nearly half of Americans believe that ghosts are spirits of the dead who haunt the living. In addition, many say that ghosts must be something otherworldly or we would not be so frightened of them. Surely, believers argue, our instincts are telling us that ghosts are an external threat, not something that comes from the mind of the believer. But so far, no one has been able to prove that the human spirit survives death—and 80 percent of Americans believe that such proof will never be found, despite scientists' best efforts. Paranormal activity may be destined to remain mysterious and unexplained—perhaps forever.

CHAPTER 1

Communicating with Spirits

One night in 1997 a young woman named Kelly received a phone call from someone claiming to be her boyfriend, Jerry. The caller asked her to meet him at a nearby park. The voice on the phone sounded exactly like his, so she agreed to go, but before she could leave, Jerry arrived at her door. He denied having called her. The couple decided she had been the victim of a prankster.

The next night Kelly received a similar phone call while Jerry was at work, and this time the caller—who again sounded exactly like Jerry—cursed her for failing to meet him at the park. Kelly knew Jerry would never talk to her like this, but after hanging up, she phoned him. She wanted to make sure he had not just talked to her, and again he confirmed that he had not made the call.

Two hours later the caller phoned again and said he needed

to see her in person. Determined to find out who was harassing her, she agreed to meet with him just down the street from her apartment, where she could watch for him from the safety of her window. Close to midnight she spotted someone she thought was Jerry at the appointed spot, and when she waved to him he waved back. She rushed outside to talk to him, then realized that he was wearing unfamiliar clothing and had a different haircut. He looked like someone from the past, perhaps around the time of World War II. Kelly turned away from the imposter and raced back to her apartment building just as the real Jerry pulled up in his car. At that moment the specter howled and disappeared.

A Ghost's Intent

In recounting this experience to ghost expert Brad Steiger, Jerry said, "Whatever this thing really was, it tried to contact Kelly just once more, about five days later. Kelly thought for sure she was talking to me until 'he' asked her to drive out to the park and meet me for a picnic after work. . . . Kelly knew that I knew that her car was in the garage for a few days. She screamed at the false Jerry to leave her alone and never to call again. And, thank the Lord, he never has."[10]

Steiger says that neither Jerry nor Kelly has a theory regarding why the entity wanted to speak with her. What message did it want to deliver in person? Or did it have something more sinister in mind?

In this case the intent of the spirit—or whatever the entity was—is unknown, but sometimes a specter appears for a clear reason. This is what occurred in June 1975, when a navy officer named Stanley encountered an old girlfriend, Karla. Stationed on a destroyer moored at Virginia Beach, Virginia, Stanley was working at his desk when he heard knocking on his door. He opened it to find Karla standing in front of him, dressed in a white nightgown, looking upset.

Seeing her torment made Stanley feel guilty, because several months earlier he had broken off his engagement with her to marry someone else, and he had done this by letter rather than in person. But Karla told him she forgave him. "I knew that you were right in doing what you did,"[11] she said. She wished him well with his new love, then walked out the door.

A few minutes later, when Stanley told a night watchman what had happened, the man told him he must have been dreaming because no woman could have slipped aboard the ship unseen. But Stanley was sure he had been awake. So he began to think that something supernatural had been responsible for the experience. He decided to write to Karla to find out whether she was all right. "I wanted to know if she might be ill, or if she might have been thinking intently of me at the time that her image had appeared in my office aboard the destroyer,"[12] he subsequently reported to Steiger.

When he received a reply to his letter from Karla's mother, the truth was more disturbing: Karla had died in a car crash at around the same time Stanley encountered her on his ship. Moreover, shortly before she died, she had told her mother that her biggest regret was that she had never responded to the letter Stanley sent her breaking off their engagement. She wished she could tell him, she said, that he had made the right decision.

Mental Mediums

There are many stories of the newly dead saying goodbye to loved ones. In Jeff Belanger's book *Our Haunted Lives*, for example, he tells of several such spirit visitations, including that of a grandmother who visited her grandson in 1971, a mother who visited her

Ectoplasm

Ectoplasm is a substance associated with spirit communications. In 1894, French physiologist Charles Richet coined the word *ectoplasm* (from the Greek words for *outside* and *something formed*) to refer to a third arm that Italian medium Eusapia Palladino apparently materialized on her body while speaking with spirits. Other nineteenth-century mediums produced ectoplasm as well, though it could take many forms. It might be a foul-smelling smoke, for example, or a gelatinous goo or rubbery blob. Today, ghost hunters primarily see ectoplasm as a mist, a fog, or an orb of light.

Regardless of the form it takes, ectoplasm is thought by some to be an essential component of spirit communication. It is said to provide an energy source that spirits need in order to move objects, make noises, or produce other forms of paranormal activity. Once the spirit leaves, the ectoplasm typically vanishes. However, in cases where the ectoplasm has not vanished, paranormal researchers have discovered it to be fake. A supposedly ectoplasmic hand that materialized during séances in the 1920s was actually a sculpture carved from a piece of liver. Skeptics cite this event as proof that all ectoplasm is fake, but believers argue that only fake ectoplasm is left behind after a séance.

daughter in 2002, and an aunt who visited her nephew in 2005. In addition, there are instances in which someone receives a spirit message without actually seeing the deceased. In such cases the person might sense the presence of a spirit or hear a song on the radio, for example, that seems to have been sent by the spirit.

There are also individuals who communicate with spirits professionally. Generally known as mediums or psychics, these people claim to receive messages from the dead that are intended for others rather than for themselves. The most prominent professional mediums working today, such as John Edward and James Van Praagh, say these messages come into their minds while they are in the presence of people wanting to talk to deceased loved ones. During this transference of thought, the medium typically remains fully conscious and is able to relate the message in his or her normal voice.

Sometimes the messages are so general that the medium might be talking to anyone about anybody. Other times the messages are so specific that the audience is convinced the medium really is communicating with the spirit being sought. For example, on John Edward's TV show *Crossing Over*, which aired from 1999 to 2004, Edward often confirmed the identity of a spirit by talking about the health problems the person had in life. He might say, for example, that a particular spirit was communicating distress in the stomach area only to be told by the deceased's loved ones that this individual was once plagued by ulcers.

However, skeptics say that mediums come up with such information by observing audience members carefully and talking with them in ways that subtly reveal facts about the deceased. Skeptic Joe Nickell explains, "The 'psychic' can obtain clues by observing dress and body language (noting expressions that indicate when one is on or off track), asking questions . . . and inviting the sub-

ject to interpret the vague statements offered."[13] As an example of the latter, if a medium says, "I see some sort of problem with the throat," a wife might say of her deceased husband, "Yes, he died of throat cancer," or she might say, "Oh, he used to cough a lot." Either way, the medium can nod and say, "Yes, that's what I thought."

Physical Mediums

Mediums who work in this way are known as mental mediums because their spirit communications only involve thought. In contrast, the communications of physical mediums feature physical signs that the spirit is present. For example, before delivering a message, a physical medium might go into an unconscious state, or trance, and seem to speak in the deceased's voice. Some physical mediums not only talk like the deceased but walk like him or her, copying mannerisms as well as speaking style. Such mediums usually call themselves channelers, saying they are channeling—or acting as a conduit for—the spirit. That is, they claim that they can allow spirits to physically possess their bodies in order to communicate directly with loved ones.

Physical mediums sometimes work in front of large audiences, but more typically they contact spirits in a more intimate setting known as a séance. This word is derived from the Old French word for "to sit." Séances are gatherings during which a medium—physical or mental—sits at a table, usually in a dark room, with one or a few people eager to communicate with spirits. Scholars disagree on when the first séances were conducted, but they were especially popular during the nineteenth century, particularly after the founding of a religion called Spiritualism, which focuses on spirit communication.

At these early séances, the presence of physical mediums often produced dramatic paranormal activity. For example, accord-

An 1887 newspaper illustration captures the scene of a séance, in which a group of people, holding hands, conjure up the spirits of dead friends or family. A guitar levitates (right) while a spirit (center) writes a note to the participants.

ing to some reports, at a séance held by medium Nettie Colburn Maynard in 1863, a piano rose, or levitated, off the floor while she was playing it. Present at the time was President Abraham Lincoln, and some accounts of the incident say that he climbed on or leaned on the piano, trying unsuccessfully to push it down. Later Lincoln said that the levitation was evidence of an "invisible power"[14] at work.

Spirit Operation

Levitation was a common feature at séances from this period, although it was usually the table around which participants sat that rose during the event. However, Spiritualists say that not all spirits move things around in order to communicate with people. Instead, some want merely to move things around. For this reason, the website of the First Spiritual Temple, a group founded in 1883 as part of the Spiritualism movement, differentiates between a spirit whose main purpose during a séance is to communicate and a spirit "who uses a medium for the intent of working with and/or manipulating energies or energy systems."[15] It calls the former a spirit communicator and the latter a spirit operator.

The website goes on to explain how a spirit operator's energy manipulation works: "Physical mediumship involves the manipulation and transformation of physical systems and energies. The spirit operators . . . are causing something to happen upon the Earth plane. What it is that actually happens varies with the style of mediumship involved, but the results can be seen and heard by others."[16]

Rapping

One of the most basic ways that a spirit manifests itself through sound is by rapping. Among mediums, rapping is defined as any sort of bang, thump, bump, knock, or the like that seems to have intelligence behind its rhythms, patterns, or responses to questions. These sounds can be faint or loud, and they can seem to emanate from walls and doors and sometimes even windowpanes and tree bark.

One of the earliest mentions of paranormal rapping was in the ninth-century manuscript *Rudolf of Fulda*. In this case the people who heard the knocking considered it to be a warning that someone was about to die. This view prevailed for centuries, until a case of rapping in the nineteenth century convinced people that the noises were not a harbinger of death but the sounds of a spirit trying to communicate.

The Fox Sisters

This case of rapping centered around two of three sisters, Kate and Maggie Fox, the first spirit communicators to be called mediums. In the late 1840s these girls—both under the age of 16 (their exact age is unknown)—started hearing strange noises after moving into a new home in Hydesville, New York. Their mother, Margaret, heard them as well, as had at least two people who had lived there previously, and she decided they were caused by a ghost. "The noises were heard in all parts of the house," Margaret later wrote. "My husband stationed himself outside of the door while I stood inside, and the knocks came on the door between us. We heard footsteps in the pantry, and walking downstairs; we could not rest, and I then concluded that the house must be haunted by some unhappy restless spirit."[17]

The Fox sisters decided to try to communicate with this spirit. When a noise occurred, they knocked on a table, and soon the unseen presence was knocking back. The sisters then began asking the presence a series of yes-or-no questions, telling it to answer yes by knocking three times or no by remaining silent. When this method of communication worked, they tried reciting the alphabet and having the presence knock when it wanted them to write down a certain letter. In this way, they received more detailed messages and learned that they were communicating with the spirit of a peddler who had been murdered five years earlier and buried in the cellar of their house.

By this time, the sisters' relatives and neighbors knew what had been going on at the Fox house, and townspeople dug up the cellar in search of a skeleton. A few human bones and some hair

Electronic Voice Phenomena

Electronic voice phenomena (EVP) are faint, often unintelligible voices heard on electronic devices at times when those voices should not be there. They might be detected within radio or phone static, for example, or on a tape or digital recording made in a quiet room. The voices only occur, however, when there is some other kind of sound already on the device, like a crackle, a hum, or—in the case of the first known recording to exhibit EVP—birdsong taped in the countryside. This has led experts in the paranormal to suspect that whatever is speaking must be manipulating the other sounds on the device in order to communicate.

The first person to discover and write about EVP was Swedish filmmaker Friedrich Jürgenson in the 1960s. Jürgenson believed that the voices belonged to spirits of the dead because one of the voices he heard sounded like his dead grandmother. Many others believe the same thing, especially since they have heard the voices say things like, "Save me!" Some people, however, say that the voices are coming from outer space or from the subconscious mind of someone with psychic abilities. Still others have suggested that this phenomenon might be caused by magnetic fields or distortions in radio waves and that any recognizable "words" heard within these sounds are the product of the listener's imagination.

were apparently found at the site. (Modern skeptics insist that the existence of bones was nothing more than a rumor. However, 56 years later, in 1906, the *Boston Journal* reported that more bones had been found in a wall of the house.) Research uncovered the fact that a peddler named Charles B. Rosna had indeed stayed at the house five years earlier. No one was able to track him down, but no evidence of murder surfaced either.

Frauds or Genuine Spirit Communicators?

Meanwhile, the Fox sisters had become local celebrities and were making money as mediums, claiming they could contact not just the spirit in their house but others as well. Under the guidance of their older sister, Leah, they not only held séances for private groups but gave public demonstrations before large, paying audiences. Both types of appearances featured rapping and other sounds by unseen spirits. A committee that was formed to determine the source of these mysterious sounds decreed that the girls could not be faking them.

Maggie ended most speculation about the veracity of their claims in 1888 when she confessed that she and her sister had been making the sounds themselves. They had done so by popping their toe and finger joints, a skill she demonstrated in front of witnesses. A newspaper reporter later wrote, "She slipped off one of [her] low shoes and placed the foot covered by only a black stocking on the sounding board. There became a succession of raps loud enough to be heard by everyone."[18]

Today some people believe that although Maggie could make noises this way, she had also really been communicating with spirits. These people say that her so-called confession was meant to hurt her sister Leah, with whom she had been feuding. (By this time Leah was claiming to be a medium, too, and had written a book about her experiences.) A year later Maggie retracted her confession, but the damage to the Fox sisters' reputation was done. The public had decided that the girls were frauds.

Mediums

By the late 1800s many other physical mediums had become suspect as well. Consequently, some began conducting séances while tied up so they could not be accused of popping joints like the Fox sisters. Other attempts to stave off accusations of fraud involved a device called the spirit cabinet, which was used by physical mediums whose séances featured a variety of physical effects. The medium was locked in the cabinet throughout the séance to show that there was no way he or she could have moved around the room in the dark to cause these effects.

Nonetheless, physical mediums were still caught faking the paranormal activity apparent in their séances. One of the most famous such fakes was Henry Slade, the first physical medium to use a popular device called a spirit slate. The spirit slate was a chalkboard that would be sealed up blank, then opened a few moments later to display a written message from the spirit world. After achieving fame through his use of the slate, Slade was caught with a tiny piece of chalk hidden between his toes. He denied that this had anything to do with the spirits' writings, but few people believed him.

Despite attempts by skeptics to denounce all mediums as fakes, mediumship still survives, and there are even communities dedicated to promoting it. The most prominent is Lily Dale, a Spiritualist community established in Chautauqua County, New York, in 1879. Because the religion of Spiritualism was inspired by the Fox sisters' activities, Spiritualists hold these women in high esteem. In fact, in 1916 their house was moved to Lily Dale.

Over 20,000 people visit this site each year, although the building itself burned down in 1955. The community is also home to nearly 300 Spiritualist mediums and healers, many of whom help visitors contact deceased loved ones.

Ouija Boards

Mediums at Lily Dale also lead workshops that teach people how to contact spirits on their own. But one of the most popular ways for nonmediums to contact spirits is not taught at Lily Dale. In fact, it does not require special instruction at all. It involves the use of a physical mediumship tool called a Ouija board. Now trademarked as a game currently marketed by Hasbro Inc., the board has its origins in the beginnings of the Spiritualist movement.

During the nineteenth century, when physical mediums like the Fox sisters asked spirits to knock a certain number of times to indicate yes, no, and the letters of the alphabet, someone developed a device that made this process easier. The device became known as a *planchette*, which in French means "little plank." The planchette is a flat-topped, three-legged plank just big enough for two people's fingertips to rest upon.

The planchette, which has a point on one end, is used in conjunction with a board on which are printed the letters of the alphabet, the numbers one through nine and zero, and the words *yes*, *no*, and *goodbye*. Users ask the spirits a question, and the planchette, or pointer, slides along the polished surface of the board to indicate certain letters, numbers, or words. Users insist they themselves are not moving the pointer with their fingertips, but skeptics say that they must be, perhaps subconsciously.

Some stories attribute the Ouija board's invention to a coffin maker who wanted to talk to the dead. Some say he named the board *Ouija* because *oui* and *ja* mean "yes" in French and German,

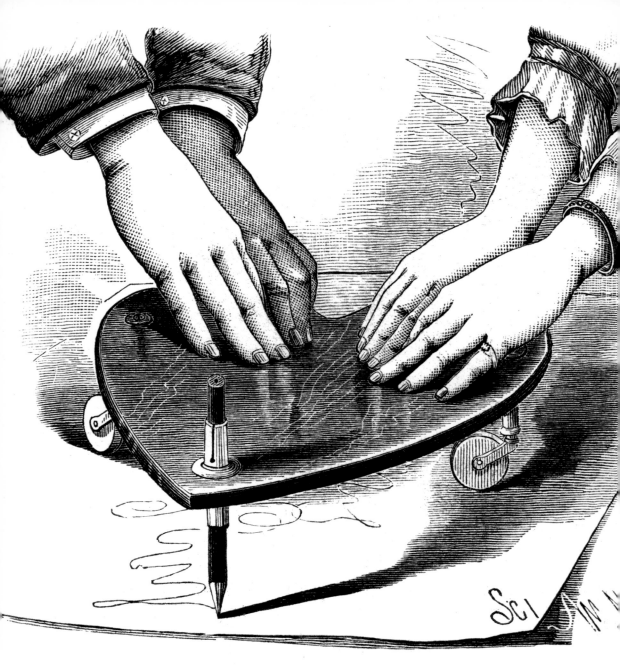

An 1885 illustration from the magazine Scientific American *depicts two people resting their fingertips on an early planchette. By guiding the movement of the planchette, spirits are supposedly able to communicate with the participants.*

respectively. Others say he mistakenly believed that *Ouija* was Arabic for "lucky." In any case, in 1892 a man named William Fuld came into possession of the board, filed a patent on it, and began commercially producing it as a novelty item. His company later sold the rights to the board to a game company called Parker Brothers (which is now owned by Hasbro).

Dangerous Messages

Although the Ouija board is marketed as a game, Spiritualists say it might not be safe for kids to use. They contend that there is no way to know exactly what kind of entity is communicating through the board. Moreover, there have been cases of people being physically or mentally harmed by the spirits they connect with via the board.

One example of such a case is cited in Stoker Hunt's book *Ouija: The Most Dangerous Game*. He tells the story of a famous recording artist, Sally (not her real name), who initially used the board as a fun way to learn gossip. She would ask the spirits about what her friends and associates were doing and thinking, and some unseen force would make the pointer move to spell out answers to her questions. Later she would confirm that the information she received from the entity was accurate.

Then, Hunt reports, Sally started receiving advice from the entity, and she did whatever it told her. He explains:

> The Ouija voices assumed the guises of various religious leaders of great stature and led the star down a pathway of destruction. Despite a serious medical condition, Sally was told by the board to stop taking her necessary medication. Although terribly afraid of heights, Sally was persuaded to

climb a dizzyingly steep nearby cliff. Soon she was coaxed to "Come to our side!" In an attempt to comply, Sally attempted suicide.[19]

Vulnerable People

As bad as Sally's case sounds, even worse things have happened as a result of spirit communication. Experts, including some psychologists, caution certain individuals against using the Ouija board. They warn that some who use the board are not connecting with spirits. Instead, they are connecting with their own subconscious, and that potentially dangerous personalities, or alter egos, may surface while using the Ouija board.

According to Hunt, drug users and people with emotional disorders or other health problems should not use a Ouija board. He states, "A state of poor health often increases suggestibility. This lowering of the operator's ability to analyze and criticize emerging Ouija messages must be clearly understood as disadvantageous."[20] Hunt also says that anyone who believes in Satan and demons should not use a Ouija board because such beliefs "almost guarantee a negative Ouija experience."[21]

By "negative experience," Hunt means something much more distressing than just raps on a table. People who dabble in spirit communication are sometimes unable to detach themselves physically or mentally from the entities they believe they have contacted. Such entities might not be the spirits they claim to be. Rather, some experts in paranormal activity say, they might be demons.

Psychic Lorraine Warren warns that attempts to communicate with spirits always involve the risk of encountering a demon. She says that mediums "may believe they are communicating with grandma or Aunt Nellie or dead rock stars, but . . . in many cases

Psychics warn that those who dabble in spirit communication may find themselves in touch with demons rather than the loved ones they sought to reach.

what comes through in the guise of human is actually inhuman, an entity that has waited for the opportunity to attack."[22]

Warren also suggests that if a deceased loved one wanted to communicate with still-living friends and family, that spirit would rely on a simple, visual visitation. She explains, "If someone we once knew and loved and liked is going to come through, they will reach us on a level that is easiest for them. That would be at the dream level, or they would come through as a visitation apparition. . . . Typically they appear once or twice and never ever again."[23]

In other words, the spirit of a loved one would not offer predictions or share gossip through a Ouija board. Such a spirit also would not engage in paranormal activity involving rapping, levitation, or other physical effects. And if this is the case, then whenever this type of paranormal activity occurs, both professional and amateur mediums would be wise to question its source, in order to guard against being deceived or even harmed by evil forces.

CHAPTER 2

Possessed by Spirits

On a Christian goth website called Godscare, a woman identifying herself simply as Connie recently shared a horrifying experience that began with her use of the Ouija board when she was 18. At first she used it with a friend, and messages provided by the movements of the pointer seemed like nonsense. Then her friend declared she did not want to use the board anymore, but Connie continued alone. Shortly thereafter the pointer spelled out clear messages.

"The board told me that a spirit came to me through the board," Connie reported. "The spirit said it was to be a friend who was to protect me from the dangers in life. It would guide me to a better life because it knew the future."[24] Connie believed the spirit was telling the truth, and from then on she spent more and more hours communicating with the unseen entity and following its advice.

After a year of this, the spirit suggested it would be easier to communicate if Connie let it speak with her voice whenever she was alone. "I permitted the spirit to speak through me. I let it use my voice and words started to form. At first gibberish then other words."[25] Sometimes when it wanted her to leave the company of others so it could speak, her fingers would tap on things uncontrollably.

After several months of this, the entity's messages turned to curses and demands that Connie kill herself. At this point, she says, "I wanted the spirit to leave. It would not go. The spirit became more aggressive and would fight for control of my voice. I would be talking and sometimes the spirit would speak. . . . My hands and arms moved overly fast sometimes. I could not sleep peacefully. The nightmares began of creatures chasing and laughing at me. I slept with a knife under my pillow."[26]

Then Connie's father said he saw a demon in the house and chased it until it dove out a window. This frightened Connie enough to call on God for help and to study the Bible to learn what words to say to fight evil spirits. Over time, with prayer and meditation, she says she was able to fight off the spirit and regain her sense of self.

Protective Energy Fields

Connie's case of possession was different from that of mediums and channelers who invite spirits to enter them temporarily in order to share positive messages or heal people. She was a victim, and the spirit who possessed her was malevolent. Ouija expert Stoker Hunt says he is aware of many such cases. "It may be difficult for most of us to accept the notion of evil spirits that take a fancy to our body and minds. It may seem too much like the theme of many late-night class-B horror movies or cheap science

Paranormal Activity

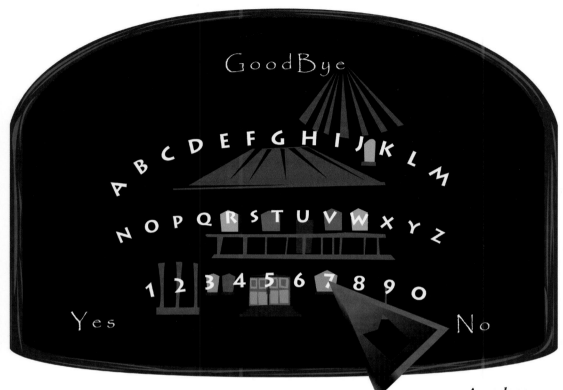

A modern Ouija board contains letters, numbers, and the words good-bye, yes, and no. Some users tell of threatening spirits entering their bodies through the board.

fiction paperbacks. But there is no doubt about the reality of invading spirits in the minds of those [who have experienced it]."[27]

Hunt reports that many experts in the paranormal believe that the human body has a natural protection against invading spirits. These experts, he explains,

> believe that we are protected from these entities by a halo of light and color—an energy field that surrounds the bodies of all living things—an aura that can be discerned by many psychics. . . . [Ex-

perts] say that the aura and the life of an individual are inseparable—and that . . . once the protective emanation—the aura—is split or entangled, the invading entity can undermine its would-be victim and create a sense of dependency within him.[28]

Hunt also reports that such entities often encourage their victims to drop all their friends, engage in reckless or dangerous behavior, and do things that jeopardize health. In addition, invading spirits want to frighten their victims as much as possible, which sometimes requires violent paranormal activity. For example, they might throw objects around, damage homes, or physically attack people. They might also show the victim horrifying images. "If fear will allow the invader to overwhelm the victim," Hunt says, "then fear it will be. The strategy is to make the victim believe that opposition to the invader is useless. When the victim finally believes that resistance is futile, the possession is complete."[29]

The Need to Hide

Another feature of possessing entities is their need for secrecy. As in the case of Connie, who was possessed after using a Ouija board, many victims say their spirit urged them to be alone as much as possible. This is so no one will try to help the victims, and also to make it easier for the entity to trick people. David Considine, a demonologist and founder of a group called Phantasm Psychic Research that is devoted to helping victims of paranormal activity, explains:

> In its larva (beginning) state, [the entity] will not show itself for what it truly is. It may present itself as a ghost—a little girl ghost, let's say. It has pa-

tience way beyond human endurance and it waits until the family starts accepting it into its life as that harmless little girl ghost, and then it starts changing. Doors start banging; the little girl ghost is gone now. It never was a little girl. The diabolical works on human recognition and tries to gain a stronghold in the person's family or the family's way of thinking. Once the phenomena start to occur it has that stronghold necessary to start to destroy that family.[30]

A Hooded Figure

This is also what typically happens in cases where a demon possesses a house rather than a person. Someone moves in to the house and encounters what is believed to be a harmless spirit, only to discover later that it is instead something evil. This was what happened to Randy and his daughter Cindy, who recount their story in Brad Steiger's book *Real Ghosts, Restless Spirits, and Haunted Places.*

When they first moved in to their house, Cindy saw a spirit that seemed to be an old man wearing a hooded cloak. He would simply appear, look at her, and disappear. Once he was accompanied by a small creature that looked somewhat like a cat, but it did not seem any more menacing than the man. Then she began hearing unintelligible voices at night, and shortly thereafter an especially cruel voice bellowed, "Cindy, show yourself to me!"[31]

Meanwhile, although Randy did see the old man once, on at least four other occasions he says he encountered a different apparition—or maybe the same one in a different form: "a black, floating, swirling mass, about four feet high and three feet wide, and [it could] change shape."[32] This entity was definitely not

harmless. Randy says, "I would wake up sometimes and feel it sitting on my chest, choking me. I actually felt it when I grabbed it and threw it off of me. When I got out of bed to confront it, it disappeared into a wall."[33]

The entity also engaged in violent paranormal activity throughout the house, knocking pictures off of walls, tossing objects to the floor, and cracking a mirror. At this point Randy and Cindy decided they had to move out. "I wasn't afraid of it," Randy insists. "But we decided to move after a month or so to keep all of our furniture from being smashed to pieces by this thing."[34]

The Amityville Horror

A more extreme example of a demon causing trouble for a family is the case of the Amityville Horror. Many people doubt this case is real; the head of the family, George Lutz, later admitted he had exaggerated aspects of his experience in publicizing it. However, he and his wife, Kathy, both passed lie-detector tests while recounting the basics of their story, and George went to his grave insisting that a demon really had nearly destroyed his family.

The Amityville Horror began in December 1975, when George, Kathy, and Kathy's three young children by another marriage moved in to a house they had purchased in Amityville, New York. A year earlier a man named Ronald DeFeo had murdered his entire family in the house: his parents, two brothers, and two sisters. But this did not worry the Lutzes—until strange things started happening there. Open doors and windows suddenly closed, closed ones inexplicably opened, and George heard band music but could not find its source. Flies kept showing up in one room—sometimes hundreds at a time—for no apparent reason, and foul smells came out of nowhere.

Even more frightening, the family later said, the face of a devil

Necromancy

Using incantations and rituals to bring forth the spirits of the dead is called necromancy. Unlike mediumship, this calling of spirits is not about communicating with them but about controlling them, usually to bring power to the necromancer. However, sometimes the necromancy results in the spirit entering the practitioner's body. Practitioners typically claim that the spirits they bring forth are spirits of the dead or elemental spirits that are neither evil nor good. Others say that necromancy always brings forth demons or other agents of the devil—or even the devil himself—who might be tricking the necromancer into thinking they are not evil.

One of the most famous necromancers, John Dee, feared that he had been tricked this way. In 1583 in England, after studying the occult, he started practicing necromancy and, he later claimed, raised spirits of the dead. He then summoned what he thought were angels and communicated with them extensively. In 1587, however, an angel calling himself Madimi asked him to do something immoral, and after he complied, Dee became afraid of what it would convince him to do next. Dee eventually decided that the angel was in fact a demon and quit practicing necromancy altogether.

appeared in their window, the devil's footprints appeared in the snow outside their house, and ghosts appeared in various rooms. One of the children claimed that a ghost pig with glowing eyes had been visiting her at night, and George claimed that he felt possessed at times by an evil spirit. A priest who came to bless the house at the Lutzes' urging said he felt an evil presence in the house. His blessing failed to drive away this presence. Instead it became even more threatening, levitating Kathy and making her appear to other family members as though she were an ugly old woman.

Finally the Lutzes abandoned their home, and just a month later the media became involved in their story, even going so far as to televise a séance held in the house. The Lutzes also coauthored a book on their experience with author Jay Anson. The book, *The Amityville Horror*, was published in 1977 and made into a movie in 1979. By this time, people had begun to suspect that the Lutzes' story might be false, especially since an investigator into the paranormal discovered that there was no snow when the family claimed to have seen the devil's footprints. Moreover, after a new family moved into the house, no other instances of paranormal activity were reported.

Still, researchers who studied the house shortly after the Lutzes moved out believe that some sort of paranormal activity really did happen there. In fact, some have suggested the same activity was responsible for the murders that occurred before the Lutzes moved in. George Lutz once said of Ronald DeFeo: "There's no doubt in our mind that he was influenced by that house and that he was controlled at least for a point."[35]

Mary Pascarella is one of several psychics who participated in investigations of the house after the Lutzes went public with their experiences in early 1976. Although no further paranormal activity has taken place there since then, Pascarella says, "The house is deceptive. . . . The energy in that house remains. It may take a hundred years . . . but it will implode again. That house is purely evil."[36] She is suggesting that the Amityville house is lulling people into thinking it harmless, so that it will once again be able to attack an unsuspecting victim.

Law enforcement personnel remove one of the bodies found in 1974 at the Amityville, New York, home of Ronald DeFeo. DeFeo was later convicted of murdering six family members—and the house in which the gruesome events took place was said to be haunted.

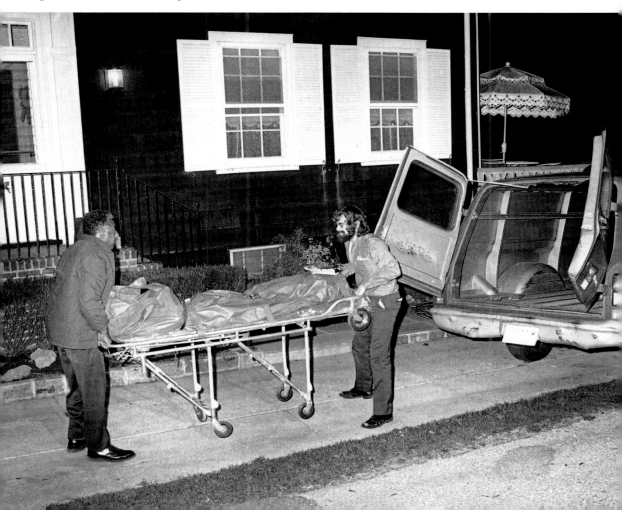

Troubled Spirits

Believers say that because demons are so deceptive, it is often hard to tell whether the entity possessing a house is a demon or a ghost. In both cases such a possession—also called a haunting—can involve paranormal activity. Like demons, ghosts can slam doors, throw objects, moan, and produce other frightening effects. But whereas demons are said to be motivated purely by evil, troublesome ghosts are believed to be acting out because of negative emotions carried over from their time on Earth.

In fact, Hunt says that most spirits trapped on Earth are "frustrated and angry." He adds, "Earthbound spirits are, most frequently, those who led troubled, destructive lives on earth. . . . It is this negativity that prevents most earthbound spirits from understanding or accepting that they are indeed dead."[37] Many people believe that in addition to negative emotions, the pain experienced during a traumatic death clings to the spirit as well. This might be why sites where violent murders have taken place are often said to be haunted.

The Murder Castle

One such site is the spot where a house known as the Murder Castle used to stand. Located in Chicago, Illinois, this house received its nickname in the late 1800s. It was then that police discovered that its owner, who called himself Henry H. Holmes but was actually named Herman W. Mudgett, had been imprisoning, torturing, and killing people—primarily women—inside the building for four years.

Holmes had specially built the structure to contain these people. It had 60 rooms, many without windows, as well as hidden staircases, secret passages, torture chambers, a gas chamber, and a basement with a crematory, acid vat, and lime pits so he could dispose of the bodies of those he had killed. He eventually confessed to killing 28 people, but judging from bones found at the site it was most likely more.

Shortly after the horrors of the Murder Castle were exposed, someone blew it up. Police suspected the culprit was a Holmes accomplice. He apparently wanted to destroy evidence that might lead to his being caught and hanged, as Holmes was. But police never proved this. The property where the Murder Castle once stood remained undeveloped for years. Nonetheless, the spot gave people an uneasy feeling, even if they did not know what had happened there.

Then in 1938 a post office was built on the site, and workers there could barely stand to be in the place. They heard inexplicable noises, sensed unseen presences, and experienced feelings of anguish, misery, or fear, perhaps picking up on the emotions of Holmes's victims. Moreover, dogs barked at the building as they went past it—if their owners could even make them go past it. Many refused.

Consequently, many people say the site is haunted. They also say that Holmes's spirit continued to kill people after he was executed in 1896. Witnesses at his trial, the trial judge, the superintendent of the prison where he had been held, the priest who visited him prior to his hanging, and several others associated with the case died in sudden or mysterious ways. For example, the foreman of the jury was accidentally electrocuted by telegraph wires. The detective who had arrested Holmes nearly died, after being struck down by an unknown illness. At the time, it was said that he had almost been a victim of the Holmes curse.

Ghostly Grief

Another example of a haunting associated with murder concerns England's Samlesbury Hall, but here the ghost expresses grief

and longing rather than misery or revenge. In the sixteenth century the hall was home to a devout Catholic family, the Southworths. When Protestant queen Elizabeth I assumed the throne, the family fell out of favor at court even though they hid their religious practices. During this period Lady Dorothy (or Dorothea) Southworth fell in love with a Protestant from the De Hoghton family. Both her parents and his forbade the match, but the lovers continued to meet in secret and planned to run away together. Before this could happen, however, Dorothy's brother killed her fiancé and buried him on the grounds of Samlesbury Hall.

Dorothy supposedly died elsewhere, at a convent in another country, after being driven mad with grief. For centuries people have reported seeing her sobbing ghost, known as the White Lady, at various places within Samlesbury Hall. She has also been seen crying and moaning as she walks toward the spot where her lover was killed. When she reaches the spot, a young man appears, wailing as well, and the two lovers embrace before disappearing.

Unfinished Business

Some ghosts apparently attach themselves to a site where they have unfinished business. One example of a place possessed by this kind of spirit is a ground-floor apartment on Charles Street in the Greenwich Village section of New York City. Ghost expert Hans Holzer encountered this ghost one Halloween while visiting the apartment with a medium named Sybil Leek.

According to Holzer in his book *Ghosts: True Encounters with the World Beyond*, the ghost first came to the attention of the apartment's occupants when a houseguest sensed the spirit's grief. This guest, named Adriana, "had been awakened in bed by a rather violent push of her arm. At the same time she felt herself compelled to burst into tears and wept profusely, although there

Henry Holmes, born Herman W. Mudgett, was hanged in 1896 for imprisoning, torturing, and killing dozens of people in a house in Chicago that came to be known as the Murder Castle. Many believe that the site of the house, which no longer stands, is haunted.

was no reason for it. Somehow she partook of another person's feelings, involving a great deal of sorrow. This happened several nights in a row."[38] Meanwhile, the person who had taken the apartment, Barrie, felt as though he were being watched, and one night he saw a white mist that convinced him a spirit was present.

Holzer was able to talk to this spirit, who spoke through the medium's voice, and he discovered that in life it had been a woman named Miss Boyd. The spirit also told him that she was looking for paperwork related to the ownership of the house in 1866. A friend of Barrie's named Elizabeth subsequently discovered, through historical research, that the building had been bought by someone named Samuel Boyd in 1827, and in 1866 a woman named Mary Boyd was charged rent in order to live there.

When the medium again contacted the spirit and asked her about this, she confirmed that she was Mary Boyd and said, "Find the paper, find the paper! This is my house!"[39] Holzer explains: "The paper, it appeared, was in the name of her father, Bill, and the landlord did not have any right to the house according to the ghost. That was the reason for her continued presence there."[40] In other words, Mary was upset that someone else had claimed ownership of the building and charged her rent to live there, because she knew the place belonged to her. Further research proved that this was indeed the case. Apparently, Mary's father, William Boyd, had filed paperwork transferring ownership to his daughter and given it to Mary. Holzer believes she lost it.

In any case the paperwork was no longer important, and Holzer communicated this to the ghost. He says, "I tried to explain that much time had gone by, and . . . I asked Miss Boyd to let go of the house and join her equally dead relatives on the other side of life."[41] After this no more signs of the ghost's presence were evident.

Possessed Objects

Miss Boyd appears to have left the apartment she possessed, but other spirits refuse to abandon what they have claimed. This is true not only for possessed people and houses but also for possessed objects. Experts in the paranormal say all kinds of things can be taken over by spirits—toys, musical instruments, furniture—and often the object remains possessed until it is destroyed.

In an online article titled "True Stories of Haunted Possessions," Stephen Wagner reports on a few such objects. One of them is a door that came from a demolished house. At night it would sometimes give off the sound of loud pounding—until the man who had taken it chopped it into bits and burned it.

Steiger reports on another possessed object: an old sofa. In August 1996, after moving into a house in which the sofa had been left behind, Patricia Emminger would see a dark shadow near or on the furniture whenever she was up at night alone. After she told her husband, Gary, about this and he laughed about it, Patricia could sense that the spirit was furious, and soon there was paranormal activity in the house to support her impression: Windows and drapes shook inexplicably, and objects were knocked onto the floor by unseen hands.

Even more frightening, the couple's four-year-old son, Mark, sometimes spoke hatefully, using words that sounded like they were coming from someone else. Eventually, Patricia became convinced that the ghost had come from the sofa and was now trying to possess her son instead. To prevent this from happening, one night she and Gary took the sofa to a deserted spot and set it on fire. After this all paranormal activity in their home ceased.

Ordinary Explanations

Steiger suggests that ghosts attach themselves to people, places, and things out of a desire to hold onto the world of the living. He also says that the spirits most prone to do this are those from individuals who indulged themselves with earthly pleasures when alive or those who were consumed by intense hate. He explains, "Hedonistic or vengeful discarnate spirits refuse to allow the natural order of spiritual progression and their evolution to higher levels of awareness to ease their desires, pain, and anger. They wish only to return to the world of the living. These disembodied entities will seek out vulnerable humans to whom they can attach themselves."[42]

The ancient
Sumerians believed
that all diseases
were caused by
demons who
had possessed
the sufferer.

Skeptics dismiss such theories as ridiculous. They deny the existence of ghosts and the possibility that a house can be haunted or possessed. Any paranormal activity that causes objects to move, they insist, is simply due to natural phenomena, such as a strong wind or the shifting of a house on its foundation. In his online book *The Skeptic's Dictionary*, Robert T. Carroll says:

> Many people report physical changes in haunted places, especially a feeling of a presence accompanied by a temperature drop and hearing unaccountable sounds. They are not imagining things. Most hauntings occur in old buildings, which tend to be drafty. Scientists who have investigated haunted places account for both the temperature changes and the sounds by finding sources of the drafts, such as empty spaces behind walls or currents set in motion by low frequency sound waves. . . . Some think that electromagnetic fields are inducing the haunting experience.[43]

Carroll also scoffs at suggestions that ghosts, if they exist, would become attached to a particular person, place, or thing. In discussing haunted houses in *The Skeptic's Dictionary*, he says, "It is not clear why demons or ghosts would confine themselves to quarters, since with all their alleged powers, they probably could be anywhere or everywhere at any time. If they really wanted to terrorize the neighborhood, they could take turns haunting different houses."[44]

Believers counter that ghosts do not confine themselves to particular locations but instead are confined there by outside forces. Just because we cannot identify or understand these forces, they

A Haunted Airline

Most ghosts attach themselves to just one person, place, or thing but in rare cases a ghost will haunt several people, places, or objects. This was the case with the ghosts of Eastern Airlines Flight 401, which crashed in the Florida Everglades in December 1972. Not long afterwards, passengers and crew members on other Eastern flights began seeing the ghosts of two men killed in the crash, Captain Robert Loft and Flight Engineer Donald Repo. Often these ghosts looked so solid that people mistook them for living people—until the apparitions vanished.

On most of these occasions, the ghosts appeared in connection with a possible airplane safety issue. For example, in one case the flight engineer reported an electrical problem before vanishing. In another, Captain Loft gave the customary preflight instructions to passengers regarding seatbelt use. Eventually, Eastern officials realized that the ghosts were appearing only on planes in which parts salvaged from the crashed plane had been used for repairs. Once these parts were removed, the ghosts stopped haunting the airline.

say, is no reason to deny their existence. They reject Carroll's condemnation of anecdotal evidence, which he says is "always incomplete and selective" and "is often passed on by interested, inexperienced, superstitious parties who are ignorant of basic physical laws."[45] This position ignores the reality that some of those providing anecdotal evidence are serious researchers into the paranormal. Even though these people can only tell ghost stories at this point, they hope one day to prove that what they've experienced is fact rather than fiction.

CHAPTER 3

Attacked by Spirits

In July 2006 a woman named Yolanda in Germantown, Pennsylvania, reported that her 14-year-old daughter, Tiffany, had been attacked at around 10:30 p.m. while sleeping—but the girl's attacker was invisible. Yolanda later said, "I heard her screaming, 'Get off of me!' I ran into her room to find her lying in the dark, shaking and trembling. I asked her what happened and she said that someone was beating her. She had scratches all over her arms. I knew no one was in the house but us two."[46]

A police officer told Yolanda that her home had once been a notorious drug house, where five people, on five different occasions, had died of a drug overdose. Once she heard this, Yolanda became convinced that the unseen attacker had been a ghost, even though she had seen no apparition. A ghost, she said, would explain other mysterious things that had been going on in the house prior to the attack: "No matter how hot the house was, no matter what the season was, the back room was always cold . . . [and there were] footsteps and . . . shadows moving from the bathroom to the back room from time to time."[47] After deciding the house had to be haunted, Yolanda and her family moved away.

Bruises and Slap Marks

According to J.J. Lumsden, an experimental parapsychologist, about 15 percent of ghost encounters involve physical attacks that leave visible marks. Besides scratches, the most common are bruises and slap marks. An example of the latter occurred to Rex Tennel in India in the summer of 2010. Tennel reports that while on vacation in the village of Ratangarh, he awoke suddenly at 2:00 in the morning feeling as though he had been slapped. But because there was no one else in the room, he convinced himself that he had been dreaming. The next morning, though, he discovered physical evidence of the assault. "I woke up and saw that one of my cheeks was wounded, like someone slapped me really hard,"[48] he says. Villagers subsequently told him that he had been attacked by the ghost of a woman—the victim of murder—who often wandered the village causing problems.

A more dramatic attack, this time resulting in odd bruises, happened in July 1996 to Sonya Donohue of Loleta, California. As she was coming down the steps of a church, a ghost threw her so far and so hard that when she hit her head she lost consciousness. She says, "The feeling of hands grabbed me on each side of my arms, turned me around . . . and threw me at least 25 feet, over grass, a sidewalk, a gravel road, and slammed me down at the outer edge of the gravel road."[49] A pool of blood formed beneath her head. The next day she discovered purple bruises on both arms. They were in the exact locations where she felt a ghost had gripped her, except that they were "not really fingerprint marks, but feathered."[50]

Hard Shoves

Being shoved down a flight of stairs is one of the most common types of ghost attack. However, there is usually no physical evi-

A ghostly vision can be more than just a sighting. Experts in paranormal activity say some ghost encounters involve physical abuse such as scratching, bruising, and slapping.

dence that a ghost has been involved in the fall. Instead, it simply looks as though the victim stumbled while trying to walk down the stairs—but the victim knows otherwise.

One example of such an incident occurred in 1982 at a restaurant in Rockledge, Florida. This restaurant (then named Gentleman Jim's, now called Ashley's) is said to be haunted by a ghost murdered on nearby railroad tracks in the 1920s. The restaurant is known for experiencing mild paranormal activity such as swaying lamps and strange noises. One time, however, the ghost apparently pushed a customer down the stairs. "I felt a huge shove against my back,"[51] the customer, Melanie S., says. She insists that at the time, there was no one behind her, even though she sensed a presence there.

Similarly, people sometimes report being shoved off chairs by an unseen force. This was a feature of a haunting reported in 1970 to police in St. Catharines, a city in the Niagara region of Canada. The incident took place in an apartment occupied by a couple with two sons aged 8 and 11. When furniture and other objects started moving on their own, the family contacted city authorities. They suspected that something was wrong with the foundation of their building. City engineers inspected the place but found nothing wrong. Consequently, the couple called the gas company, then the fire department, and next the people in charge of public utilities to see whether some other aspect of the building's structure was to blame. Again, nothing was found to be wrong.

But objects, including heavy furniture, kept moving on their own. So when the mother of the family, Barbara, noticed some police officers responding to a call elsewhere in the apartment building, she decided to ask them into the apartment to witness the paranormal activity. It was so startling that the officers called for a full investigation into what was happening. One of the involved officers, Constable Mike McMenamin, later said that at the outset of the investigation, "Our superiors thought we were pulling a joke on them."[52] Another, Constable Robert Crawford,

remarked, "At first I thought the family must be mental, but believe me, what I saw was not done by human hands."[53]

The paranormal activity they witnessed included photos jumping from the wall, objects tossed off a dresser, lamps falling over, and furniture raising substantially off the floor. On one occasion, Crawford came into a room to find a bed inexplicably raised 2 feet (61cm) off the floor at just one end. Then, he says, "not believing my eyes, I summoned Constable [Dick] Colledge, who was outside the apartment. On our return, the bed was in the same position, but it was now supported by two chairs."[54]

The chairs in the house were involved in a lot of other paranormal activity as well. They raised officers into the air or tossed them off their seats, and when people sat in what Barbara said seemed to be the ghost's favorite chair, they were often shoved off it by an unseen hand. Feeling this force was, for the police, one of the worst aspects of the case. "It was one of the scariest things I've ever been involved with," Constable Harry Fox later said. "At least in your normal work, if you're confronted with a big man, you can defend yourself. But this was different, unpredictable. I think it was some sort of invisible energy which you couldn't see."[55]

The paranormal activity ended as abruptly as it began, and some people said it was because one of the boys had been playing a prank and suddenly got tired of it. But the police, who had also suspected one of the boys at first—especially because he was present when most of the activity took place—had watched carefully for signs of a prank and found none. "After all those weeks and all those incidents," Fox said, "not one of us thought it was trickery."[56]

Focused on One Person

It is not unusual for authorities to suspect a prankster in cases where one person is always or almost always present when the

Capturing Spirits

Modern ghost hunters typically use a great deal of equipment while investigating a haunting. For example, they use electromagnetic field detectors to register energy fluctuations and digital thermometers to detect subtle drops in room temperature. Either of these events could be caused by a ghost's presence. They also use advanced audio and photographic equipment, including infrared (night vision), thermal (temperature sensitive), and digital video cameras, to record sounds and images of things that humans present cannot hear or see.

Few of the images captured look anything like a ghostly human figure. Far more common are orbs, which are round spheres of light. Some of these are normal by-products of faulty photography, but others—especially those with vapor trails—are said to depict the human spirit. Images of haze or fog are said to depict the spirit as well, while images of mist shaped like a funnel—called vortexes (or vortices)—are said to represent a portal between the worlds of the living and the dead. Cameras have also captured images of dark shadows moving around rooms. Some ghost hunters call these "shadow people" and say they are the souls of the unenlightened or lost.

paranormal activities occur. It is also not unusual for one person to be the focus of the unseen force causing the activity. In fact, in some cases the unseen force physically attacks just one person in the household.

One of the most famous examples of this occurred in 1878 to a family in Amherst, Nova Scotia. The family consisted of Daniel Teed; his brother John; Daniel's wife, Olive; Olive's siblings Esther, Jennie, and William; and Daniel and Olive's two young children. Also living in the house was a boarder, Walter Hubbell.

The place experienced no paranormal activity until shortly after Esther, then age 19, was molested by a shoemaker in the town. Then Esther and Jennie began hearing and seeing strange things in their room at night: bedcovers moving inexplicably, noises coming from a closed box of fabric, the box moving of its own accord. Soon Esther was physically affected as well; one night she awoke to find herself choking and her skin feverish and puffy, but her swelling went away after loud banging came from underneath the bed. Still, she stayed in bed, and when a doctor visited her, more banging came from under the bed, and Esther's pillow and bedding moved on their own.

Next the doctor heard scratching, and when he looked up at the wall above the bed he saw a message scraped in the plaster: "ESTHER COX YOU ARE MINE TO KILL."[57] From this point on, the paranormal activity escalated throughout the house. An unseen force threw silverware, set fires, shoved furniture, and more. It also attacked Esther, sticking pins in her cheeks, slapping her, and stabbing a small knife into her back.

Even when she tried going elsewhere, the paranormal activity continued. Sometimes—like when she went to church—the force simply banged on things. At other times it was more violent. After Esther began working at a farm, its barn burned down, and the townspeople held her responsible, sentencing her to four months in jail. She was let go after only a month, though—whereupon the paranormal activity lessened and soon stopped. She was never troubled by ghost attacks again, and her story might have been forgotten had not Hubbell written a book about it, *The Great Amherst Mystery*. In it he included signed statements from 16 people who had witnessed the paranormal activity surrounding Esther Cox and insisted it was exactly as Hubbell had described it.

Poltergeist Events

Experts in the paranormal call this type of paranormal activity a poltergeist experience. The word *poltergeist* means "noisy spirit" in German, and today it is typically used to refer to cases where a young person, usually a teenager, becomes the focus of attention for an unseen attacker that produces a large number of physical effects. As Lumsden explains, "Outbreaks typically involve object movement and/or inexplicable noises within a specific environment. Sometimes incidents can have an almost playful character or nature to them, whilst at other times they can be perceived as more hostile."[58]

The attacks usually begin after the victim has undergone some sort of emotional trauma, and they end nearly as abruptly as they began. "Generally speaking," Lumsden says, "most poltergeist outbreaks don't seem to last particularly long, and normally persist for somewhere between a couple of weeks and a couple of months (although some have been reported to last, on and off, for years)."[59]

The victims of this type of paranormal activity are usually adolescents or children on the verge of puberty or, less often, adults who are going through emotional stress. These similarities led researchers in the 1950s to suspect that the reason for the activity could be found not in the spirit world but in the victim. Specifi-

The Drumming Poltergeist

One of the best documented written accounts of early poltergeist activity is the case of William Drury. He is described in the 1682 book *Saducismus Triumphatus* by Joseph Glanvil, chaplain to King Charles II of England. In 1661, Drury was arrested for banging noisily on a drum while begging. The magistrate who had him jailed, John Mompesson, kept the drum. A month later he heard its sound echoing through his house in the middle of the night. But when Mompesson checked the drum, no one was touching it.

The mysterious drumming continued every night thereafter, even after Mompesson destroyed the drum. Other noises were soon heard as well, including scratching and scrabbling. Mompesson's children and servants insisted that an unseen entity had hit, pushed, pinched, or yanked on them. As the violence escalated, Drury was released from jail, committed other crimes, and was arrested again. This time Mompesson had him charged with witchcraft. Drury was acquitted of this charge but after being convicted of stealing a pig he was deported to America on a prison ship. As soon as he was gone, the strange phenomena at Mompesson's house stopped.

cally, parapsychologists have theorized that the victims of poltergeists possess a psychic ability known as psychokinesis.

Psychokinesis

Psychokinesis, or PK, enables a person to move things through mental power alone. Scientists disagree on whether this ability actually exists, because controlled studies have been inconclusive. Believers, however, note that it is possible that being monitored in a laboratory is unsettling enough to make it difficult for test subjects to use their psychokinetic ability. If PK does exist, though, the type of PK that might be responsible for the poltergeist phenomenon is RSPK, or recurrent spontaneous psychokinesis, because it happens over and over again without warning.

At the forefront of research into RSPK was parapsychologist William Roll, who began studying poltergeist cases in the 1960s. He determined that poltergeist cases typically occur in places with magnetic fields, such as near geologic faults. He also found that far more girls than boys are the focus of poltergeist cases and that many of them were secretly happy that their home was being attacked. Roll theorizes that this is because most young people have no way to express their anger without getting into trouble, and a poltergeist allows them to be blameless for the ghost's tantrums.

Roll studied over 100 poltergeist cases in developing his theories. However, some people say there might be hundreds more. In his article "How to Survive a Poltergeist," Stephen Wagner says, "It is unknown how common poltergeist activity is. Certainly, remarkable cases in which household objects are tossed about are relatively rare. But those are the cases that get attention and are documented simply because they are remarkable, especially if the activity persists over many days.... There may be many more cases, however, that occur just once or on rare occasions to people."[60] As examples of such cases, Wagner cites times when an object inexplicably tumbles to the floor or a picture falls off a wall when two people are expressing anger toward one another. At such times, Wagner says, these things would probably be dismissed as coincidence, even though a poltergeist might be to blame.

Skeptics vs. Believers

Skeptics argue that events blamed on poltergeists are nearly always the result of actions by pranksters. Teenagers love to play pranks, which explains why so many poltergeist cases involve teenagers. One of the most prominent skeptics, James Randi, also insists that it is nonsense to believe that poltergeists, ghosts, and psychic abilities are real. In his book *The Poltergeist Phenomenon*, Michael Clarkson says of Randi, "His theory about life is that Nothing is Amazing, except for science and things that can be proven without a doubt. In Randi's world, if you didn't see it happen, it likely didn't happen. And even if you saw it happen, someone could have duped you."[61]

Randi says that belief in ghosts and poltergeists and other unproven paranormal phenomena is dangerous because it makes people susceptible to scams and unnecessary emotional distress. Belief in the paranormal, he contends, can "cripple our perception of the world around us." He adds, "We must reach for the truth, not for the ghosts of dead absurdities."[62]

Believer Wagner counters that "there is ample documentation that poltergeist activity does take place, in various levels of severity and for various lengths of time."[63] He suggests that there are too many examples for all of them to be labeled as pranks. He believes that psychic abilities are responsible for these events, and he advises people confronted with this kind of paranormal

In some belief systems, spirit attacks are a sign that the victim has become too materialistic and the attacks will end if the victim becomes more spiritual.

activity to consider who in their family might be causing it. "Who in the household is exhibiting signs of stress?"[64] he asks, suggesting that the person under stress be treated with compassion.

Wagner also recommends patience in addressing the problem. Lights turning on and off, furniture and other objects being moved around, and toilets flushing are usually temporary and not dangerous. "If the [paranormal] activity seems mild and harmless, it might be best to wait it out,"[65] he says.

Elemental Entities

Many ghost hunters believe that spirits and not PK are responsible for poltergeist activity. For example, the 17 experienced ghost hunters employed by Wexford Paranormal say on the team's website that it is odd that people would suggest that poltergeists are not ghosts. Still, they accept the theory that poltergeist activity is connected to intense emotion. They also acknowledge that it is possible that a nonhuman entity—an elemental entity—could be responsible for the paranormal activity instead of the spirit of someone who once lived. They add that "regardless of the differing options, poltergeists are very real and are the most destructive type of paranormal activity."[66]

Entities that play with televisions and light switches are not what the ghost hunters are referring to when they comment on the destructive nature of poltergeists. They are most likely referring to events such as those that took place at Borley Rectory in the 1920s and 1930s. Unlike the Amityville case, where researchers into paranormal activity only became involved after the physical events had ceased, the Borley Rectory was subjected to serious study while the poltergeist was still active. In fact, it was the focus of some of the earliest scientific research into such hauntings.

The Borley Rectory

This work was done in the 1930s by noted psychical researcher Harry Price, one of the first people to investigate paranormal activity using scientific methodology. When he heard about a haunting at the Borley Rectory, just northeast of London, he launched a long-term study of the site, living there with a team of researchers from 1937 to 1938.

Prior to Price's arrival at the old manor, which had been built in 1863, residents had seen an apparition on several occasions,

Before it was demolished in 1944, the Borley Rectory was considered the most haunted house in England—and possibly the world. Noted paranormal researcher Harry Price did an extensive study of the activities reported to be occurring at the site.

both at night and during the day. On one of these occasions, four people witnessed the apparition at the same time. Many people had also heard mysterious footsteps, whispers, and other inexplicable noises in the house. They believed they were dealing with the spirit of a nun, because a local legend told of a nun who was executed after she had broken her vows and tried to run away with a lover. According to this legend, the nun had been buried within the walls of a building that was said to have stood on the site centuries earlier.

After Price began his study, paranormal activity at the rectory escalated. People were inexplicably pelted with rocks. The rocks seemed to appear out of nowhere, and they sometimes abruptly changed direction in midair. Price also heard the unexplained sound of ringing bells and saw objects move for no apparent reason.

Along with his team of researchers, he took careful notes, measured the distance that various objects traveled, and tried to photograph the apparition. During his investigation, he discovered messages scrawled on walls. They were addressed to Marianne Foyster, the wife of the rectory's minister. The messages expressed confusion and told Marianne to get help.

Price also found a woman's skeleton beneath the floor of the basement. During a séance conducted at the rectory, he received a message that the dead woman was indeed a nun and that she had been killed in 1667 by her lover. Price concluded that this was the identity of the apparition, a troubled spirit unable to move on to the afterlife. However, he felt that the messages addressed to Marianne and the rock throwing were not caused by the spirit of the nun. Instead, he believed that their source was a poltergeist connected somehow to the minister's wife. When she moved out of the house, the poltergeist activities ceased—which seemed to confirm Price's suspicion. But others have noted that the poltergeist activity did not begin until Price moved in to the rectory, and the rock throwing only took place when he was present. Could Price have been the focus of the poltergeist instead of Marianne? Or was he always present because he was actually faking the paranormal activity? People who have studied the case disagree strongly about which is true, even though there is no evidence that Price was a fraud.

Controversial Evidence

People also disagree strongly about the photograph that Price put forth as evidence of an apparition at the Borley Rectory. It shows a hazy area that he said was a ghost; many now believe it was smoke from a nearby fireplace. But as a psychical researcher, Price had sometimes revealed other people's ghost photographs to be fake. For this reason his supporters doubt he would have created a fake photograph. They also say he would have thoroughly examined such an important piece of evidence.

Skeptics counter that people like Price, who arrived at the rectory already believing in ghosts, see what they expect to see. However, skeptics also see what they expect to see regarding ghost photographs: fakery. To them the apparition in a photograph has always been manufactured by the photographer, either accidentally through poor camera skills or on purpose as part of a plan to dupe people.

Ironically, ghost hunters also advise approaching evidence of paranormal activity with skepticism. For example, on the website of the Southwest Ghosthunters Association, a list titled "Rules to Follow in an Investigation" cautions ghost hunters: "Arrive with skepticism. Maintain an open mind and be aware that there may be a natural explanation for what is going on. Always know what to look for and remember to try and prove that the place is not haunted first, before accepting that it is paranormal in origin."[67] Many other ghost-hunting organizations advise this approach as well, because it is important for them to get at the truth of a paranormal experience. Without the truth, they say, they will be unable to help people suffering from paranormal attacks.

CHAPTER 4

Chasing Away Spirits

I n March 2011 a family in Coventry, England, reported that for several months they had been experiencing poltergeist attacks so violent and so frightening that they needed to call experts in to help them get rid of the entity. Their experience began with lights turning on and off. Next silverware inexplicably jumped out of drawers, and other objects flew across rooms and smashed against walls. Then they discovered one of their dogs dead at the bottom of the stairs. When the vet told them there had to be extreme force involved in the fall, they became convinced that the entity had pushed their pet. Now they were terrified that the entity would kill them as well.

"Things have got so bad my kids are now seeing a counselor,"[68] the 34-year-old mother of the family, Lisa Manning, said. Several times the family fled the house while the poltergeist activity was going on, but because they were poor and living in government housing, they soon had no choice but to return. They asked the government to move them to a different house. This request prompted an outcry from skeptics who believe the family fabricated a poltergeist in hopes of being moved to a nicer location. In an effort to prove their case, the family videotaped some of the paranormal activity; the tape did indeed show objects moving seemingly unaided.

Both Fake and Genuine

Many people believe these images were faked. In fact, Chris Jensen Romer of the website Polterwotsit, which examines poltergeist cases with a critical eye, says of Manning's videotape, "It has to be the most unconvincing thing I have seen in a long time. . . . Of course genuine things can appear faked, but everyone I know [who has seen it] has fallen about laughing, and, well it's a bit like the movie *Paranormal Activity*. Yet clearly Lisa Manning to my mind seems to think she is haunted."[69]

Experts say that faked evidence is not unusual in poltergeist cases. Author Michael Clarkson says there can be "instances of fraud and genuine paranormal activity *within the same case*."[70] Usually this happens when the paranormal activity does not happen as expected, right when the victim wants witnesses to believe it is real.

Clarkson provides a hypothetical example of such a circumstance:

> Let's say a young boy unconsciously causes objects to move with his mind. Police, family members, and parapsychologists all testify to the legitimacy of the events because they have all been closely watching the boy and rule out trickery. But genuine

poltergeist events seem to be fleeting and difficult to produce. And so, his abilities may start to wane. . . . [By now he] may have become enamored with all the attention he had been getting, and doesn't want to give up the center stage.[71]

In this situation, the victim might resort to pushing a chair when no one is looking, for example, or rigging something to fall seemingly unaided.

Unfortunately, when the supposed victim of spirit attacks is caught cheating even once, it makes the entire case suspect. Even worse, reporters can label the person a liar, and that label can stick. As Clarkson notes, "Although the media is sometimes quick to embrace a poltergeist story for its unusual qualities and potential human-interest angles, journalists can also turn against a case at the slightest hint of a hoax. That was true even in the more superstitious times in the early 20th century."[72]

Moreover, throughout the history of paranormal research, a single hoax can cause people to condemn the entire field of paranormal research. Hans Driesch, in his book *Psychical Research: The Science of the Super-Normal*, confirms this. Thanks to hoaxes, he says, "there are journals [from the early twentieth century] that empty whole buckets of sarcasm as soon as psychical research . . . is so much as mentioned, without having made any attempt even to glance at the serious literature of the subject."[73]

Cleansings

In the case of the Coventry haunting, the media only found out about Lisa Manning's story and labeled the tape a hoax after her local housing authority decided to take action. Believing the tape to be genuine, the housing authority sent a priest to her house

A pitcher of holy water (pictured) and prayers are sometimes used to cleanse a building of evil spirits. The ritual, usually performed by a member of the clergy, does not always put an end to mysterious paranormal activity.

to try to rid it of the spirit. The priest performed a Catholic and Anglican ritual known as cleansing, whereby holy water is sprinkled in various locations and prayers are said with the intent of driving the spirit away. Similar cleansings are also performed by people of other faiths. For example, some Native Americans use the smoke from a burning bundle of sage to purify a dwelling (a process called smudging), then ask the spirit to go in peace.

However, a cleansing did not end the paranormal activity at Lisa Manning's house—nor did five additional cleansings. After each time, the activity subsided, but then it started up again. This is the part of Manning's story that led Romer to conclude she really believed she was being haunted. Romer writes:

> Assuming she has not read the more technical literature on [poltergeist] cases, she would be unlikely to know this is a strongly recurring motif in the literature. It's not something psychics or spiritualists would think to mention [to her]—but a lull of a few weeks, or up to three months after a priest's blessing, then a recurrence of phenomena, often less intense than the original form is something we come across time and time again.[74]

Help from Mediums

Romer mentions psychics and spiritualists because this is who the family contacted for help when the cleansings failed to chase out the poltergeist. They advised the family to scatter salt around the house, to hang crucifixes on the walls, and to wear crystals—all of which are methods used for centuries to ward off spirits. One medium, Lisa reported, also told her what was causing the paranormal activity: "Our house is a portal, a kind of bus stop for spirits, which they use to pass into our world."[75]

Prominent British medium Derek Acorah, however, disagrees with this assessment. He visited the home in March 2011, shortly after Lisa first spoke with the media about her problems, and felt the presence of an angry spirit named Jim, who admitted to killing the dog. Acorah, who had his own TV show on the paranormal called *Most Haunted* from 2002 to 2005, reports that he cleansed the house through the use of candles, crystals, and a special blessing and was able to rid it of the spirit. After that the paranormal activity ceased, and Lisa rescinded her request that the government move her elsewhere.

Fatal Attempts

Some attempts to drive away a spirit end tragically. There are over 1,000 known cases worldwide of people being seriously injured or killed during such attempts, with many more cases surely going unreported. Among the most prominent examples is that of 22-year-old Janet Moses of Wainuiomata, a suburb of Wellington, New Zealand. Moses died in October 2007 during a ceremony to rid her of an evil entity.

This ceremony, called *mākutu* lifting, was once a common religious practice among the indigenous Maori people of New Zealand. (The word *mākutu* is the Maori word for "curse.") However, the government banned the practice from 1907 to 1962, so few Maori today know how to perform the ritual properly. This was the case with the people trying to cleanse Moses.

Moses's problems began a few weeks earlier, after her sister stole a concrete lion statue from a local pub. Moses started exhibiting signs of mental illness almost immediately thereafter, but because of the timing her family believed that she had been possessed by an evil entity within the lion. They therefore arranged for a *mākutu* lifting to take place at the home of her grandmother.

As part of the ceremony, the family held hands in a circle around Moses. Someone held her down as they chanted and continuously poured water over her face. As the ritual progressed, the chanters became almost trancelike. Some were so committed to completing the ritual that they ignored signs that Moses was in distress. Others felt her struggles were due to the evil entity fighting to stay within her. So they kept on with the *mākutu* lifting until Moses drowned.

In the wake of her death, five family members were tried and convicted of murder. They received no jail time but were required to perform community service. In addition, a coroner's inquest into the case declared that the death was due to the ceremony being performed without a trained Maori priest, or *tohunga*, being present. *Mākutu* lifting itself was not criticized, and it is still practiced today.

Exorcism Leads to Death

Rituals to drive away spirits or demons occur in many different faiths. Under Islamic belief, for example, rituals involving special prayers repeated over several days or weeks are performed to force an entity called a jinn to leave a person or place. In the Hindu religion, incantations, verses, and passages from holy writings are read aloud for days in order to get rid of spirits. In Judaism, entities that have become tied to a person or place are encouraged to move on during a ceremony that includes the blowing of a sacred horn, the shofar.

In the Roman Catholic faith, the ritual to drive away a spirit or demon is called an exorcism. As with *mākutu* lifting and similar practices, the most famous cases of exorcism are those resulting in fatalities. One such case is that of Anneliese Michel in Germany in 1976. Her story was the inspiration for two movies, *The Exorcism of Emily Rose* (2005) and *Requiem* (2006). Michel's exorcism occurred after she had spent time in a psychiatric hospital

Voodoo

In the oral religious tradition of Voodoo, spirit possession is a way for people to communicate with the spirit world and the gods, perhaps to ask for favors or protection in exchange for ritualistic animal sacrifice. To this end, individuals allow themselves to be possessed so that others can talk to the possessing spirit. But such sessions can be dangerous because of how completely a Voodoo spirit takes control of its host. The person's consciousness is gone, replaced by the spirit, so that the host no longer moves, talks, or thinks like himself or herself, and this can drive the possessed person permanently insane.

Consequently many Voodoo practitioners believe it is important to drive a spirit out of a possessed person as quickly as possible after the spirit's services are no longer needed. This sometimes means that after a ceremony where several people have been possessed, a large group of people must be exorcised at the same time. Chanting, drumming, and dousing with water might all be a part of exorcism rituals. In extreme cases where a spirit refuses to leave, the possessed person might be brought to the brink of death in order to drive the spirit out. In some cases, this has led to actual death, when people succumb to smothering or drowning before Voodoo priests deem the spirit gone.

for severe depression and for having hallucinations and hearing voices. Psychiatrists there gave her many drugs, but they caused her to have seizures and did not end her hallucinations.

A devout Catholic, Michel decided that she had become possessed by a demon and that only an exorcism would help her. She put in a formal request to the Catholic Church asking for one, then had a family friend take her on a pilgrimage to the town of San Damiano in Italy, the site of a holy spring. But she refused to drink from it and could not stand being near symbols of her faith, particularly crucifixes. Consequently, her friend, Thea Hein, decided that Michel was right about being possessed, and others soon came to believe this as well. Eventually, the church arranged for the exorcism to take place in secret, led by two priests: Father Ernst Alt and Father Arnold Renz.

Michel underwent 67 exorcism sessions in all during a 10-month period beginning in September 1975. A session might last as long as four hours. She did not see any of her doctors while in the care of the priests, and her depression grew worse. She refused to eat or drink, and in July 1976 she died of starvation, malnutrition, and dehydration. Afterward her parents and the priests were charged with negligent homicide.

At the trial, tape recordings of the exorcism sessions were played. The court heard Michel speaking strangely, arguing with the priests in a way that convinced some she really was possessed. Psychiatrists evaluating the evidence, however, have suggested she was probably suffering from multiple personality disorder at the time of the sessions.

Either way, the defendants were all found guilty, although eventually their sentences of six months in prison were reduced to three years' probation. The guilty verdict was, many believe, an attempt to warn other priests not to perform exorcisms, but they still take place. In fact, in recent years an increasing number of Catholic priests have taken courses to learn how to conduct exorcisms. In Italy—home to the Vatican, which is the center of the Catholic faith—there are now between 300 and 400 official exorcists, according to church officials.

A Successful Exorcism

According to believers, many of these Catholic exorcists are successful in driving away demons. One of the cases most often cited as a success is the exorcism of Roland Doe (a pseudonym probably provided by the Catholic Church). This event was the inspiration for the 1971 novel *The Exorcist*, the 1973 movie *The Exorcist*, the 1993 nonfiction book *Possessed* (in which Doe was called Robbie Mannheim), and a 2000 movie also called *Possessed*.

There are various reports of how the 14-year-old boy at the center of the case came to be possessed by an evil entity. Most say that Roland first encountered the entity in 1949 after using a Ouija board to contact a recently deceased aunt. Roland experienced bizarre incidents, including objects flying or levitating, physical attacks, and words like *hell* seemingly scratched on his skin by claws or branded there. His family thought that the initial, mildest activity was being caused by the spirit of the deceased aunt, but as it escalated they decided it was the work of the devil, so they sought help from their Lutheran minister. He declared that the boy needed an exorcism. According to some accounts, the minister performed it himself in February 1949, but because his church did not have a prescribed exorcism rite, he followed the one for the Episcopal Church. It was unsuccessful.

Roland's family then took him to a Roman Catholic priest, who performed another exorcism, this time at Georgetown University Hospital in Washington, DC (a medical facility run by members of the Jesuit religious order). This too was unsuccessful, because Roland injured and frightened the priest so badly he could not finish the rite. Consequently, the family tried another priest, the Reverend William S. Bowdern from College Church in St. Louis, Missouri. He began performing exorcism rites on Roland in March 1949 and continued through April, working primarily at night.

During this period, the boy's behavior grew extremely difficult. He cursed, raged, struck out at people, and worse. Though tied to a bed during the exorcism sessions, at one point he managed to stab Bowdern with a spring he had removed from the bed frame. Suddenly, on April 18, 1949, the boy's behavior changed.

Before starting the exorcism session that night, the priest forced Roland to put religious medals around his neck and hold a crucifix, and Roland calmly began asking about prayer. Bowdern felt the demon possessing the boy was trying to deceive him into thinking it was gone, so he continued reciting the words associated with the ritual, compelling the demon to leave. Soon the boy was flailing about, yelling and claiming to be a fallen angel. Then at around 11:00 p.m. the boy's voice changed into one that was very deep, and he cried out, "Satan! Satan! I am Saint Michael! I command you, Satan, and the other evil spirits to leave this body, in the name of Dominus, immediately! Now! Now! Now!"[76] After a convulsion, Roland said quietly, "He is gone."[77] After this, neither he nor his family was troubled again.

Skeptics argue that this is because the boy simply grew tired of faking his possession and decided to stop acting up. For example, author Mark Opsasnick, who investigates unexplained phenomena with a critical eye, says, "Personally, I do not believe [Roland] was possessed. There is simply too much evidence that indicates that as a boy he had serious emotional problems."[78] Opsasnick states that the boy hated his school, thought that his odd behav-

The movie The Exorcist, *and the book that preceded it, were loosely based on a case in the 1940s involving a 14-year-old boy who was said to be possessed by an evil entity. Pictured is a scene from the 1973 film.*

ior would get him kicked out of class, and became enraged when instead it resulted in him being trapped in bed surrounded by priests. This rage, Opsasnick suggests, is what led to the most bizarre behavior of his supposed possession. As to why the boy would even begin such a ruse, Opsasnick says, "There is no question there was something wrong with [him] . . . that modern-era psychiatry might have best addressed. [He] was not just another normal teenage boy."[79] Opsasnick blames much of Roland's psychological problems on his parents, saying, "The facts show that he was a spoiled and disturbed only child with a very overprotective mother and a non-responsive father."[80]

Fear

But where Opsasnick sees trickery, others see ghosts, and still others see psychokinesis. There are also those who think that paranormal activity is caused by fear. In his book *The Poltergeist Phenomenon*, Michael Clarkson says, "Perhaps poltergeist activity is not black magic but stress magic. . . . When you feel afraid or angry, your body goes through a whole series of chemical changes that effectively turn you briefly into a different person and give you substantial new powers."[81] Clarkson suggests that this fear produces energy which in turn can produce an altered mental state that results in paranormal activity.

Indeed, fear is a component of most encounters with the paranormal. But which came first, the paranormal activity or the fear, and how much has the media influenced the perception of the paranormal? Numerous movies have depicted frightening ghosts, demonic possessions, and poltergeist attacks. Consequently, on a dark night filled with spooky sounds, many people are more inclined to think about hauntings than psychokinesis.

Biased Points of View

Experts who have studied public perceptions related to the paranormal say that religion, too, influences how people respond to spooky sights and sounds. Those who believe that the spirit lives on after death are more likely to think "ghost" than "prankster." For the nonreligious, though, it is easier to accept the notion that human beings have hidden psychic powers than to consider that there might be an afterlife. Ghost expert Hans Holzer speaks to this when he says:

> To the materialist and the professional skeptic—that is to say, people who do not wish their belief that death is the end of life as we know it to be disturbed—the notion of ghosts is unacceptable. No matter how much evidence is presented to support the reality of the phenomena, these people will argue against it and ascribe it to any of several "natural" causes. Delusions or hallucinations must be the explanation, or perhaps a mirage, if not outright trickery. Entire professional groups that deal in the manufacturing of illusions [such as photographers and magicians] have taken it upon themselves to label anything that defies their ability to reproduce it artificially through trickery or manipulation as false or nonexistent.[82]

Those who are skeptical by nature or more focused on the material as opposed to spiritual world are not the only ones with biases. As Opsasnick points out in speaking of the case of Roland Doe:

> Each of the parties involved in this case approached it from its own frame of reference. To psychiatrists, [Roland Doe] suffered from mental illness. To priests this was a case of demonic pos-

session. To writers and film/video producers this was a great story to exploit for profit. Those involved saw what they were trained to see. Each purported to look at the facts but just the opposite was true—in actuality they manipulated the facts and emphasized information that fit their own agendas.[83]

That each person brings his or her biases to such a case is something that both skeptics and believers can agree on. Otherwise they agree on little else—just as believers disagree on various theories related to the source of paranormal activity—and it is unlikely that there will ever be a consensus on ghostly phenomena. The reason, as author Jeff Belanger points out, is that one person's truth is not necessarily another's. He explains:

> In one regard, truth is relative. Speak to any devoutly religious person about what *truth* is, and he or she will likely quote from one of his or her religious texts. He or she may believe the text and its teachings to be the truth. But is it universal truth? No, because there are a great many belief systems on our tiny planet, and so far, none of them has been able to capture 100 percent of the marketshare of believers. One *truth* doesn't speak to all people.[84]

This is the case whether those belief systems are religious or secular.

Belanger believes that once people accept the existence of paranormal activity, they will be provided with something valuable to

Herbs and Salt

One of the oldest beliefs is that burning herbs will drive away evil spirits. The type of herb varies according to the belief system but all cleansing herbs have a pleasant odor because bad smells are associated with bad spirits. Some religions use incense to chase away unwanted spirits. Others use the smoke of burnt offerings, such as fatty animal parts burned after the animal is ritually sacrificed, to ask the gods to rid an area of evil.

Many people also use salt to ward off evil spirits. Before casting a spell, for example, sorcerers might ring an area with salt so that they can stand within a circle safe from harm. Similarly, practitioners of the Shinto religion use salt to protect sumo wrestlers from the interference of evil spirits, throwing handfuls into the center of the ring before a fight to force such spirits to leave. In many cultures, it is common to toss salt over one's shoulder to drive away any demons that might be lurking nearby. In the Western world, this typically occurs after someone has spilled the salt, a custom that developed after people decided that the devil must have been responsible for the spillage.

consider. He says, "Ghosts are a sign of something else being out there beyond our traditional understanding of the world."[85] For Belanger, the thing beyond understanding concerns the nature of the human spirit, which he believes survives death. For others, the answer to the mystery of paranormal activity lies within the human mind, energy fields, or some other theory yet to be developed—and debated.

NOTES

Introduction: Frightening Forces

1. Quoted in Jeff Belanger, *Our Haunted Lives: True Life Ghost Encounters*. Franklin Lakes, NJ: Career Press, 2006, p. 156.
2. Quoted in Belanger, *Our Haunted Lives*, p. 157.
3. Quoted in Belanger, *Our Haunted Lives*, p. 157.
4. Belanger, *Our Haunted Lives*, p. 12.
5. Belanger, *Our Haunted Lives*, p. 12.
6. Robert T. Carroll, "Ghosts," *The Skeptic's Dictionary for Kids*, 2011. http://sd4kids.skepdic.com.
7. Wexford Paranormal, "Residual Hauntings." http://wexfordparanormal.org.
8. John Kachuba, *Ghosthunters*. Franklin Lakes, NJ: New Page/Career Press, 2007, pp. 30–31.
9. Kachuba, *Ghosthunters*, p. 25.

Chapter 1: Communicating with Spirits

10. Quoted in Brad Steiger, *Real Ghosts, Restless Spirits, and Haunted Places*. Canton, MI: Visible Ink, 2003, p. 550.
11. Quoted in Steiger, *Real Ghosts, Restless Spirits, and Haunted Places*, p. 166.
12. Quoted in Steiger, *Real Ghosts, Restless Spirits, and Haunted Places*, p. 166.
13. Joe Nickell, "John Edward: Hustling the Bereaved," *Skeptical Inquirer*, December 2001. www.csicop.org.
14. Haunted Museum, "Séances in the White House? Lincoln and the Supernatural." www.prairieghosts.com.
15. First Spiritual Temple, "What Is Mediumship/Channeling?," 2001. www.fst.org.
16. First Spiritual Temple, "What Is Mediumship/Channeling?"
17. Quoted in First Spiritual Temple, "The Fox Sisters," 2001. www.fst.org.
18. Quoted in First Spiritual Temple, "The Fox Sisters."
19. Stoker Hunt, *Ouija: The Most Dangerous Game*. New York: Harper & Row, 1985, p. 81.
20. Hunt, *Ouija*, p. 142.
21. Hunt, *Ouija*, p. 142.
22. Quoted in Hunt, *Ouija*, p. 73.
23. Quoted in Hunt, *Ouija*, p. 74.

Chapter 2: Possessed by Spirits

24. Connie, "Ouija Board Demon Possession," Godscare. www.godscare.net.
25. Connie, "Ouija Board Demon Possession."
26. Connie, "Ouija Board Demon Possession."
27. Hunt, *Ouija*, pp. 85–86.
28. Hunt, *Ouija*, p. 86.
29. Hunt, *Ouija*, p. 87.
30. Quoted in Kachuba, *Ghosthunters*, p. 72.
31. Quoted in Steiger, *Real Ghosts, Restless Spirits, and Haunted Places*, p. 107.
32. Quoted in Steiger, *Real Ghosts, Restless Spirits, and Haunted Places*, pp. 107–108.
33. Quoted in Steiger, *Real Ghosts, Restless Spir-*

its, and *Haunted Places*, p. 108.

34. Quoted in Steiger, *Real Ghosts, Restless Spirits, and Haunted Places*, p. 108.
35. Quoted in Steiger, *Real Ghosts, Restless Spirits, and Haunted Places*, p. 36.
36. Quoted in Steiger, *Real Ghosts, Restless Spirits, and Haunted Places*, p. 37.
37. Hunt, *Ouija*, p. 87.
38. Hans Holzer, *Ghosts: True Encounters with the World Beyond*. New York: Black Dog & Leventhal, 1997, p. 471.
39. Quoted in Holzer, *Ghosts*, p. 471.
40. Holzer, *Ghosts*, p. 472.
41. Holzer, *Ghosts*, p. 472.
42. Steiger, *Real Ghosts, Restless Spirits, and Haunted Places*, p. 111.
43. Robert T. Carroll, "Haunted House," *The Skeptic's Dictionary*, July 19, 2011. www.skepdic.com.
44. Carroll, "Haunted House."
45. Carroll, "Haunted House."

Chapter 3: Attacked by Spirits

46. Yolanda, "Invisible Attack," About.com, July 2006. http://paranormal.about.com.
47. Yolanda, "Invisible Attack."
48. Rex Tennel, "Angry Slapping Ghost," About.com, July 2011. http://paranormal.about.com.
49. Sonya Donohue, "Slammed by a Ghost," About.com, February 2010. http://paranormal.about.com.
50. Donohue, "Slammed by a Ghost."
51. Quoted in Stephen Wagner, "When Ghosts Attack," About.com, 2011. http://paranormal.about.com.
52. Quoted in Michael Clarkson, *The Poltergeist Phenomenon: An In-Depth Investigation into Floating Beds, Smashing Glass, and Other Unexplained Disturbances*. Pompton Plains,

NJ: New Page, 2011, p. 25.
53. Quoted in Clarkson, *The Poltergeist Phenomenon*, p. 25.
54. Quoted in Clarkson, *The Poltergeist Phenomenon*, p. 26.
55. Quoted in Clarkson, *The Poltergeist Phenomenon*, p. 29.
56. Quoted in Clarkson, *The Poltergeist Phenomenon*, p. 31.
57. BBC, "The Haunting of Esther Cox." www.bbc.co.uk.
58. Quoted in Stephen Wagner, "A Parapsychologist's Tale," About.com, 2011. http://paranormal.about.com.
59. Quoted in Wagner, "A Parapsychologist's Tale."
60. Stephen Wagner, "How to Survive a Poltergeist," About.com, 2011. http://paranormal.about.com.
61. Clarkson, *The Poltergeist Phenomenon*, pp. 158–59.
62. Quoted in Clarkson, *The Poltergeist Phenomenon*, pp. 159–60.
63. Wagner, "How to Survive a Poltergeist."
64. Wagner, "How to Survive a Poltergeist."
65. Wagner, "How to Survive a Poltergeist."
66. Wexford Paranormal, "Poltergeists." http://wexfordparanormal.org.
67. Southwest Ghosthunters Association, "Rules to Follow in an Investigation." www.sgha.net.

Chapter 4: Chasing Away Spirits

68. Quoted in Laurie Hanna, "Coventry Family Call Exorcist After 'Haunting' of House by Poltergeist," *Mirror* (London), March 29, 2011. www.mirror.co.uk.
69. Chris Jensen Romer, "A Coventry Poltergeist?," Polterwotsit, March 31, 2011. http://polterwotsit.wordpress.com.
70. Clarkson, *The Poltergeist Phenomenon*, p. 124.

71. Clarkson, *The Poltergeist Phenomenon*, p. 124.
72. Clarkson, *The Poltergeist Phenomenon*, p. 127.
73. Quoted in Clarkson, *The Poltergeist Phenomenon*, p. 127.
74. Romer, "A Coventry Poltergeist?"
75. Quoted in Romer, "A Coventry Poltergeist?"
76. Quoted in Mark Opsasnick, "The Haunted Boy of Cottage City: The Cold Hard Facts Behind the Story That Inspired *The Exorcist*, Part 2," *Strange Magazine*, 2000. www.strangemag.com.
77. Quoted in Opsasnick, "The Haunted Boy of Cottage City."
78. Opsasnick, "The Haunted Boy of Cottage City."
79. Opsasnick, "The Haunted Boy of Cottage City."
80. Opsasnick, "The Haunted Boy of Cottage City."
81. Clarkson, *The Poltergeist Phenomenon*, pp. 86–87.
82. Holzer, *Ghosts*, p. 24.
83. Opsasnick, "The Haunted Boy of Cottage City."
84. Belanger, *Our Haunted Lives*, pp. 11–12.
85. Belanger, *Our Haunted Lives*, p. 12.

For Further Research

Books

Debi Chestnut, *Is Your House Haunted? Poltergeists, Ghosts, or Bad Wiring.* Woodbury, MN: Llewellyn, 2011.

Mark L. Cowden, *Spirit Voices: The First Live Conversation Between Worlds.* San Antonio, TX: Anomalist, 2011.

Rupert Matthews et al., *Unseen World: The Science, Theories, and Phenomena Behind Paranormal Events.* Pleasantville, NY: Readers Digest, 2008.

Rich Newman, *Ghost Hunting for Beginners: Everything You Need to Know to Get Started.* Woodbury, MN: Llewellyn, 2011.

Brian Righi, *Ghosts, Apparitions, and Poltergeists: An Exploration of the Supernatural Through History.* Woodbury, MN: Llewellyn, 2008.

Kelli Sayed, *Paranormal Obsession: America's Fascination with Ghosts & Hauntings, Spooks & Spirits.* Woodbury, MN: Llewellyn, 2011.

Richard Wiseman, *Paranormality: Why We See What Isn't There.* London: Pan Macmillan, 2011.

Websites

American Society for Psychical Research (www.aspr.com). This website includes information on poltergeists and psychokinesis.

Committee for Skeptical Inquiry (www.csicop.org/si). This website provides access to articles from the *Skeptical Inquirer* magazine.

Ghostvillage.com (www.ghostvillage.com). This website provides information on research and evidence related to paranormal activity as well as discussion forums on ghost-related topics.

International Ghost Hunters Society (www.ghostweb.com). This website provides a wealth of information about ghost-related subjects.

Paranormal Activity Research Association (www.para4.org). This website features articles and discussions related to paranormal activity and ghost hunting.

Your Ghost Stories (www.yourghoststories.com). This site is a place where people can post their own experiences with the paranormal, in addition to reading other people's stories and learning about the subject in general.

INDEX

V

Van Praagh, James, 19
voodoo, 74
vortices, 56

W

Wagner, Stephen, 46–47, 60–62
Warren, Lorraine, 30, 32
Wexford Paranormal, 11, 62

Paranormal Activity

PICTURE CREDITS

Cover: Thinkstock/Photodisc

AP Images: 41, 45

© Corbis: 21

Fortean Picture Library: 63

© Heritage Images/Corbis: 28

iStockphoto.com: 53, 70

Photofest: 78

Thinkstock/Hemera: 35

Thinkstock/iStockphoto.com: 10

© Sandro Vannini/Corbis: 31

About the Author

Patricia D. Netzley is the author of dozens of books for children, teens, and adults. Her young adult nonfiction books include *Alien Encounters* for ReferencePoint Press. Her books for other young adult nonfiction publishers include *Alien Abductions, UFOs,* and *The Greenhaven Encyclopedia of Paranormal Phenomena.* She lives with her husband, Raymond, in Southern California.